I AM WORTHY ENOUGH
MY SETTLING DAYS ARE OVER

30 attributes of a godly man that women desire

I AM WORTHY ENOUGH

MY SETTLING DAYS ARE OVER

---

30 attributes of a godly man that women desire

YOLANDA MARSHALL NICKERSON

Copyright © 2016 by Yolanda Marshall Nickerson

Published by Glimpse of Glory Christian Book Publishing

ISBN: 978-0-9983588-0-2

Printed in the United States of America

Unless otherwise identified, all Scripture quotations in this publication are from New King James Version Study Bible. Copyright 1997, 2007 by Thomas Nelson, Inc. Some scriptures are also taken from the NIV internet version.

All rights reserved. No part of this publication may be reproduced, stored in a retrieval system or transmitted, in any form, or by any means, electronic, mechanical, recorded, photocopied, or otherwise, without the prior permission of the copyright owner, except by a reviewer who may quote brief passages in a review.

Mr. & Mrs. Larry Nickerson
Married on May 3, 2014

This book is dedicated to all the single women who have been praying to God for a husband. I want to encourage each of you by letting you know that God has heard your prayer, and He will respond at the appointed time. I decree that by the Grace of God, your husband will find you and obtain Favor from the Lord.

CONTENTS

INTRODUCTION 9

DECLARATIONS 13

1: HE LOVES GOD.. 15

2: HE IS COMMITTED TO GOD 19

3: HE OBEYS GOD 21

4: HE IS A PRAYING MAN........................... 23

5: HE IS A GREAT LEADER......................... 27

6: HE IS A GIVER 31

7: HE IS SUPPORTIVE 33

8: HE IS RESPECTFUL 37

9: HE IS FAITHFUL 39

10: HE IS COMPASSIONATE 41

11: HE IS PATIENT 43

12: HE IS HONEST 45

13: HE IS A LISTENER 47

14: HE IS CONFIDENT 49

15: HE HAS SELF-CONTROL 51
16: HE IS A PROVIDER 53
17: HE IS ACCOUNTABLE 57
18: HE IS STRONG 59
19: HE IS WISE 61
20: HE IS DRIVEN 63
21: HE IS COMPLIMENTARY 65
22: HE IS ENCOURAGING 67
23: HE IS LOYAL 69
24: HE IS FORGIVING 71
25: HE IS A VISIONARY 73
26: HE IS HUMBLE 77
27: HE IS DISCLIPINE 79
28: HE IS ONE OF A KIND 83
29: HE HAS FAVOR WITH GOD 87
30: HE VALUES YOUR WORTH 89
A PERSONAL JOURNAL 91

INTRODUCTION

When we as women do not know our worth, then we cannot value our worth. On the other hand, when we know our worth, we will value it to the fullest. And then we will find ourselves only embracing what is good for us, even as it relates to our relationships. We will no longer find ourselves settling in life.

Many of us have settled for less than God's best numerous times. Some of us have not only settled for unhealthy relationships, but nearly any and every thing else.

Many of us who have been in at least one or more unhealthy relationships told ourselves at some point that we would not succumb to another unhealthy relationship, yet we found ourselves back in that same situation again—after we told ourselves that we would not settle. I remember telling myself that more than one time, but seemingly I did not wake up and actually put my foot down until after five unhealthy relationships and two failed marriages that ended in divorce.

I was a broken woman who had low self-esteem. I did not know my worth, so I could not possibly value my worth. I was searching for love, attention and affection from men who proved that they could not offer either of them. All I received was hurt, pain, stress, confusion, and a list of other things that were contributing factors of dysfunctional relationships. Many of you have parallel stories.

If you have found yourself in what I call the "negative relationship cycle" several times, and you are ready to be free and wait for God to send you the man that He desires for you to have in your life, I can assure you that He is going to send you His "Best Man." The one who will not only marry you, but treat you the way God intends for you to be treated: like a Queen. The "Best Man" will be one whose attributes will be in alignment with God. He did it for me and I am confident that He will do the same for you, too.

I AM WORTHY ENOUGH

DECLARATIONS

"Thou shalt also decree a thing, and it shall be established unto thee: and the light shall shine upon thy ways."
(Job 22:28)

Declaration: My settling days are over! I will no longer allow myself to be hindered or stagnated by holding on to someone who I am not supposed to be connected to.

Declaration: From this day forward, I will only receive the best God has for me, in every area of my life.

Declaration: I am free and released from every soul tie.

Declaration: Lord, I am ready to receive the husband you have already handpicked just for me.

Declaration: By this time next year, I will be married.

You may use the space provided in the back of this book to write other declarations, prayer requests, and to communicate your thoughts with your Heavenly Father about other attributes you desire in a husband that may not be listed in this book; that may be equally as important to you as the 30 that are discussed in this book.

ATTRIBUTE 1

HE LOVES GOD

> *By the Grace of God, I decree that your husband will love God and love you as Christ loves the church.*

John 14:15 says, "If you love Me, you will keep My commandments." When a man loves God with all of his heart, he will make sure his life is pleasing unto Him. He will do things that will bring honor to God. He will not partake in sinful things that will impede his spiritual growth and affect his personal relationship with God.

A man who loves God...can easily love and appreciate the woman that He has made and fashioned for him. The Bible tells us the story about Adam and how God took one of his ribs while he was asleep and created woman. And then he called her Eve. (Read Genesis 2:21-22). God did not want man to be alone; that is why he created woman to be his helper. And if God loved and thought enough of a man to give him a woman made from his own rib to be his helper, then he should love her just as much as he loves himself because she is a part of him.

He knows that she is not just any woman—she is his wife, his better half, his "soul mate that was sent from

Heaven." That is the kind of man that God has for you, one who loves Him with all of his heart. And he will also love you the way you deserve to be loved when you become his wife.

I AM WORTHY ENOUGH

ATTRIBUTE 2

HE IS COMMITTED TO GOD

> *By the Grace of God, I decree that your husband will be committed to God and to you.*

When a man is sold out to God, then he will be "fully committed" to the things of Him. He knows that his commitment to God is what keeps him grounded and rooted and on the right path. He knows that he has no room to slack in carrying out his purpose. He also knows that a part of his purpose is to commit to building and providing for his family.

God blessed me with a husband who is fully committed to Him and to his family, too. When I first met my husband, I realized he was not afraid of commitment. That meant a lot to me. I was so used to dating men who were afraid to make commitments.

I now know that if a man is not committed to God, then he certainly will not be committed to a woman. But I can assure you that the man God has for you will understand what it means to commit, and he will not be afraid to commit to you.

ATTRIBUTE 3

HE OBEYS GOD

> *By the Grace of God, I decree that your husband will be obedient to God and do what is required of him.*

The Bible encourages all of us by letting us know that "we will eat the good of the land when we are willing and obedient." (Isaiah 1:19).

A man who truly understands the importance of obedience will do what is required of him. He does not even find happiness in doing things his way because he desires to submit his ways to God—in total obedience.

He knows that he can expect many good things to happen for him and his family when he walks in obedience. He also knows that God holds the man accountable for the way he leads his family, so he will strive every day to lead his family with the guidance of the Lord.

I must say that it is so much easier to tread the footsteps of a man who is following the footsteps of the Lord. If he is leading his family in the same direction that God is leading him, then his entire family will always end up in the right place at the right time. His entire family can also receive those great rewards that are released from Him for being obedient.

ATTRIBUTE 4

HE IS A PRAYING MAN

> *By the Grace of God, I decree that your husband will have a prayer life. And he will pray for and with you.*

I certainly know what it is like to have a man in your life who does not have a prayer life and one who does have a prayer life. It makes a big difference when a man is not only the leader of his family, but a praying leader who knows how to make the atmosphere change in the home as well as in other places.

A man who has a prayer life knows what it means to bombard Heaven on behalf of his family, friends, and even strangers that he may encounter on his journey. He will not so easily give up or stop pulling on Heaven with his prayers until he feels the hand of God moving. Yes, I am talking about a man who is not so quick to leave the throne room; that secret place where it is just him and the Spirit of the Lord. He does not mind spending that much needed time in prayer.

A man who prays fervently will command every single thing to line up, according to the plan that God has set for his family. He believes and stands firmly on what the Bible says in James 5:16, "The effectual fervent prayers of a righteous man availeth much."

I AM WORTHY ENOUGH

ATTRIBUTE 5

HE IS A GREAT LEADER

> *By the Grace of God, I decree that your husband will be a great leader; one that you will be proud to follow.*

God created man to be a leader and gave him qualities that will exemplify great leadership skills. Some of those qualities may consist of him being committed, wise, determined, stable, trustworthy, dependable, accountable, having an impressive and solid work ethic, having a positive attitude, etc.

A man who understands leadership knows how important his role is at home, at work, at church, etc. He is highly confident in his leadership abilities because he knows that he was created by "The Great Leader" who he trusts to lead him every day. The Bible declares that the steps of a good man are ordered by the Lord. (Psalm 37:23).

He knows that other people are not only looking up to him, but they are following him. He has the capability of making a difference by positively touching the lives of those who are around him daily. He consistently strives to bring out the best in people, especially his family.

You can trust and depend on the man that will be at the helm of your family because he has already been well-trained by God to lead the right way.

I AM WORTHY ENOUGH

ATTRIBUTE 6

HE IS A GIVER

> *By the Grace of God, I decree that your husband will be a cheerful giver; one who will willingly share with you.*

Giving was one of Jesus' greatest attributes. Look at what He did for us all! He gave His life so that we can all live our lives to the fullest. The Bible says, "…God loves a cheerful giver." (2 Corinthians 9:7).

A man who has a giving heart shows that he is unselfish. The sweet, beautiful heart of God can be seen and felt through his giving. He does not mind sharing, especially with his family. He understands that he was not only created by God to lead his family, but he is expected to give his love, time… and financial resources to his family.

A man who loves his family will not attempt to withhold anything from them because he knows that the more he gives, the more God will supply all of his needs and his family's needs according to His riches and Glory. (Read Philippians 4:19).

ATTRIBUTE 7

HE IS SUPPORTIVE

> *By the Grace of God, I decree that your husband will be supportive of what you are purposed to do and aspire to do.*

It is a blessing to have a man in your life that is honored to support you. It can be very hurtful, confusing and frustrating to have someone in your life that does not support you. I remember when I was dating this guy who was fully aware of the things that I was passionate about doing, but he was not supportive. Have you ever been in a place in your life where you felt like someone close to you was not there for you or even "cared enough" to support something you were doing or aspired to do?" If so, you know exactly what I am talking about.

I later realized that that man could not push and support me if he did not know how to. I also realized that his love and passion toward the things of God was not like mine. God also showed me that he was not the one who was purposed to support me in the things of Him.

When God blessed me with my husband, he gave me just what I needed. My husband pushes me, supports me, and prays with and for me. He does so many other wonderful things, too. He understands that we are one in the same and that is how God sees us. He also knows that when God joined us together He allowed our ministries to intertwine too.

I am certain you have aspirations, dreams, talents and gifts too, and the last thing you need in your life is a man who does not know how to push you into your destiny, or offer his support. I want you to know that you won't have to be concerned with the lack of support when God sends you the man He has for you. You can have confidence in knowing that God has already equipped, disciplined and prepared him to push you, support you…even before the two of you meet.

I AM WORTHY ENOUGH

ATTRIBUTE 8

HE IS RESPECTFUL

> *By the Grace of God, I decree that your husband will be respectful to you at all times.*

Most men who have respect for women were actually raised that way. They were taught as children how to open doors for a woman, speak kind words to her, etc., and those teachings spilled over into their adult life.

A man who is respectful will do things for his woman to show how much he respects her. He will speak kind words to her. He will take her out to really nice restaurants. He will shower her with nice gifts. He will buy her roses on any given day. He will take her on trips, etc.

He will also respect her viewpoints about certain things. He will receive her advice and wisdom on certain matters. He will value her thoughts. He knows how to humble himself and respect the God in her.

ATTRIBUTE 9

HE IS FAITHFUL

> *By the Grace of God, I decree that your husband will be faithful to God and to you—in every part of your union.*

A man with a sincere heart for God, one who is faithful to the things of God, will be faithful to the woman He has for him.

He will be faithful in taking care of her. He will be faithful in covering her in prayer. He will be faithful in building her up when she is low in spirit. He will be faithful in leading her in the ways of God. He will be faithful in honoring his vows.

A man who is faithful knows that God honors faithfulness. He knows that God will reward him for being faithful to Him and to his precious family. Matthew 25:21, "…you have been faithful over a few things, I will make you ruler over many things…"

ATTRIBUTE 10

HE IS COMPASSIONATE

> *By the Grace of God, I decree that your husband will be compassionate—sensitive to the needs of others, especially his family.*

A man who is compassionate does not only think of himself. He thinks of others, especially his family. He is very concerned and he cares about the well-being of his family. He is also sensitive to their needs and the needs of others.

He will do whatever he can to help anyone on his journey. The Bible reminds us in Hebrews 13:2 to "…not forget to show hospitality to strangers, for by so doing some people have shown hospitality to angels without knowing it." (NIV).

When a man is compassionate, he exemplifies the love of God through his "good deeds." God can trust him to feed the hungry, provide clothing to the naked, and even minister to the hurting and lost souls.

ATTRIBUTE 11

HE IS PATIENT

> *By the Grace of God, I decree that your husband will be patient and stay within God's perfect will.*

When a man knows how to wait for God to move on a certain situation that he may be dealing with, he will not step outside of His will by trying to handle that situation in his own strength. He will wait.

Isaiah 40:31 says, "But they that wait upon the Lord shall renew their strength; they shall mount up with wings as eagles; they shall run, and not be weary; and they shall walk, and not faint."

He understands that God has an appointed time for things to happen in his life. He also knows that if God has promised He will do a certain thing for him, then he can depend on Him to do whatever it may be.

When a man can patiently wait for God to move for him, then he is teaching his family how important it is for them to do the same thing, because he is at the helm of them.

ATTRIBUTE 12

HE IS HONEST

> *By the Grace of God, I decree that your husband will be an honest man; one who will do the right thing in every situation.*

A man who is honest will do what is right, even when situations and circumstances try to convince him to do the opposite. He does not practice being deceitful or manipulative. And he will not part his lips to lie about anything. He knows that one of the things God hates is a "lying tongue."

He is straightforward and honestly expresses his thoughts and concerns.

He does not mind telling a person if he cannot do something for them. And if he tells someone he is going to do something for them, he will certainly honor his commitment. He will not default on his word. He knows that being honest can help shape and build his character, and even strengthen his relationship with God.

ATTRIBUTE 13

HE IS A LISTENER

> *By the Grace of God, I decree that your husband will be a great listener; one who you can share your thoughts…with.*

I know that it is important to you (and most women) to have a loving and understanding man in your life who will listen to what you have to say without making you feel like your opinion does not matter or what you have to say is not important.

Having a man to just listen to you share your thoughts, ideas, joys…and things that may even trouble you at times is such a great feeling. I now know how it feels to have a man who will freely listen to me express my thoughts and share those important things that matter to my heart as well as those things that make me feel like complaining or giving up.

I must admit that I have not always had someone like my husband in my life. He has been such a great listener and I thank God for him. I feel like some time I talk a bit much, but he still listens to me.

I want you to know that the man God has for you will have a listening ear. He will know just how much it means to you to have him in your life.

ATTRIBUTE 14

HE IS CONFIDENT

> *By the Grace of God, I decree that your husband will have confidence in himself and in you when you become one.*

A man who is confident is not the same as one who thinks he knows it all. He is not arrogant or boastful. He is not intimidated by anyone else. He is one who believes that he is capable of being great in what God has gifted him to do.

He knows that it takes confidence to carry out his God-given purpose. He knows that it takes confidence to lead his family. He knows that he must have confidence in the decisions he makes for his family. He knows that it going to take having confidence to become successful. He knows that he has to be confident to do all that he aspires to do in his life.

ATTRIBUTE **15**

HE HAS SELF-CONTROL

> *By the Grace of God, I decree that your husband will have self-control in every situation he encounters in his life.*

I am certain that it is important to you to have a man in your life who knows how to control himself under pressure. After the experiences I had in some of my past relationships, I knew that I could not bear having another man in my life that lack having self-control. God also knew it. So He blessed me with a man who has self-control; who I am proud to call my husband.

A man who has self-control does not allow situations or circumstances to make him get out of character. He knows how to handle those situations and circumstances in a very peaceful, godly manner. He knows how to pray about those things that are out of his control and fully depend on God to stay in control. He allows God to fight all of His battles.

ATTRIBUTE 16

HE IS A PROVIDER

> *By the Grace of God, I decree that your husband will be a great provider; one who will make sure you are well taken care of.*

It is such a great feeling to have a man in your life that can provide for his family. We women feel comfort, peace, and security when we know that we have a provider in the home. There is no woman I know who wants a lazy man who cannot provide for her and their family.

A man who knows that God made him the responsible party to lead and provide for his family, then he will be accountable to his family and do what is required of him to make sure their needs are met.

In a previous marriage I was with a man who was a very poor provider. There was no sense of security for our family. He literally did not have his priorities in order. He was not a good steward over his money. He was very unwise in his spending. I would be remiss if I didn't tell you that I totally settled in that marriage. I was one miserable, unhappy woman.

I am proud to say that I now have a man in my life who is a provider and a wise great steward over his money. I want you to be confident that God has the perfect man for you who will be honored to provide for you and his family.

I AM WORTHY ENOUGH

ATTRIBUTE 17

HE IS ACCOUNTABLE

> *By the Grace of God, I decree that your husband will hold himself accountable for his actions, mistakes and decisions.*

It is one thing for someone else to hold you accountable, but it is another thing when you can actually hold yourself accountable. When a man takes full responsibility for holding himself accountable for his actions, mistakes, decisions, it shows a lot about his character.

He is definitely the kind of man that you need to have in your life. He is not one who shifts the blame on someone else for something he did that produce negative results. He will not make any excuses for something he did wrong. He will not try to hide and cover up what he did. He will accept responsibility and do what is needed to make it right.

ATTRIBUTE **18**

HE IS STRONG

> *By the Grace of God, I decree that your husband will be strong; one who will take charge and lead with authority—in a loving and kind way.*

I do not know any women who desire to be with a man who is soft, timid and weak. Most women want to feel the protection and strength from their man.

A man who is strong understands what it means to take charge and lead his family in a loving and kind way. He knows how to take authority and set order in the home, make tough decisions for his family, etc.

He knows that his strength comes from the Lord and that his family is holding on to his strength. He will not crumble when his family goes through a fiery trial. He will stand firm and depend on God just like Shadrach, Meshach and Abednego did when they were thrown in a fiery furnace that was seven times hotter than the normal temperature. (Read the full story in book of Daniel-Chapter 3).

ATTRIBUTE 19

HE IS WISE

> *By the Grace of God, I decree that your husband will use wisdom in every aspect of his life.*

God is the One who grants wisdom to man. The Bible declares,"…the wisdom that comes from heaven is first of all pure; then peace-loving, considerate, submissive, full of mercy and good fruit, impartial and sincere."

Being that God appointed man to lead his family, it is critical that he use wisdom in every aspect of his life. With the chaos, confusion, turmoil and negativity going on in the world today, you cannot by any means afford to have a man in your life that cannot operate and run his household with the wisdom of God.

He has to know how to make wise decisions so that his precious family can benefit greatly from the outcome and not emotional decisions that can easily make his family suffer from the outcome. He has to lead with wisdom at all times.

ATTRIBUTE 20

HE IS DRIVEN

> *By the Grace of God, I decree that your husband will be driven and use the talents and gifts God bestowed upon him.*

A man who is driven does not find comfort in being lazy. He does not find pleasure in just sitting on his rear end. He is determined and motivated to do his best. Even on a day he is not feeling his best, he will ask God for strength to get up and do what needs to be done for his family.

He is honored and grateful to use the gifts and talents God has bestowed upon him. He is one who will take advantage of every opportunity that God gives him.

ATTRIBUTE 21

HE IS COMPLIMENTARY

> *By the Grace of God, I decree that your husband will compliment you; one who will make you feel special, loved, desired...*

I do not know a woman who does not like to be complimented by her man. I love to hear my wonderful husband compliment me. It certainly makes me feel special, loved, desired, appreciated, etc.

Most, if not all, men know that women love to be complimented. A man who appreciates the woman God has blessed him with will compliment her often.

The one that God has for you will tell you that you are beautiful. He will tell you that you look amazing in the dress you desire to wear for a dinner date. He will tell you he likes the way a certain hair style looks on you. He will even compliment you when you don't feel like you look your best.

ATTRIBUTE 22

HE IS ENCOURAGING

> *By the Grace of God, I decree that your husband will be encouraging; one that can speak life into you at all times.*

We all need to be encouraged on our journey in life. Encouragement can quickly take us from a place of hurt and pain to a place of peace and happiness. I am certain that you feel much better after being encouraged. It helps brightens your day and puts a smile on your face, doesn't it?

How much more meaningful would it be to hear words of encouragement from your man—the one that God has for you. It is a blessing to have a man in your life who knows how important it is to encourage you just as much as you encourage those around you: family, friends, etc.

A man who understands your need for encouragement will speak loving and kind words to your mind, spirit and soul often. He knows how to lift you up during the toughest of times. Even when you feel like throwing in the towel, he knows how to motivate you to keep pushing toward your destiny.

ATTRIBUTE 23

HE IS LOYAL

> *By the Grace of God, I decree that your husband will be loyal to you and that he will see the greatness in you.*

It is a great thing to have a man in your life that is loyal. A man who is loyal will do the best he can for you. He cares about you and what matters to you. He will not give up on you. He will be there until the end, even if others leave your side.

He will gladly pick you up when life's situations knock you down. He will even speak up for you and defend you in situations where you are not able to speak for yourself and defend yourself.

A man who is loyal believes in you. He sees greatness in you and helps bring it out of you. He does not mind helping you in any way that he can.

ATTRIBUTE 24

HE IS FORGIVING

> *By the Grace of God, I decree that your husband will have a forgiving heart; one that will be quick to forgive someone...*

A lot of men are known for holding anger and grudges in their hearts. If someone does something to hurt them, they immediately go into an attack and payback mode.

But a man who has a forgiving heart knows the godly way to pay back anyone for hurting him is to forgive them. He knows his blessings can be placed on hold if he does not forgive. Therefore, he will not allow anything or anyone to block him from receiving the blessings that God has for him and his family.

He also understands that if he harbors the seed of unforgiveness in his heart, it can manifest itself into sickness, oppression, depression, fear, and so many other things that can easily have an adverse effect on his life, and his family's life too.

ATTRIBUTE 25

IS A VISIONARY

> *By the Grace of God, I decree that your husband will be a visionary; one who will always do what is in the best interest of his family.*

According to Merriam-Webster's dictionary, "A visionary is having or showing clear ideas about what should happen or be done in the future."

God gives the man the vision for his family because he is the head of his family. Since God puts the man in charge, he is expected to do what is required of him as the visionary.

He knows how important it is to look ahead with his spiritual eyes when making plans for his family. He knows that he must pray before he finalizes his plans to ensure they are in alignment with the plans that God has for his family.

He knows that he is responsible for making every decision for his family, including the major decisions. Some major decisions include purchasing a new home and a new car, taking an expensive vacation, making certain investments, etc. He steers away from making emotional or abrupt decisions for his family because he knows that those kinds of decisions can have an adverse effect on his family.

He knows that if he makes a decision that is not in the best interest of his family, a decision that produces negative results, he will accept full responsibility because he knows that God is holding him accountable for every decision that he makes for his family.

The visionary that God has for you will need your love, support, and motivation when you all are joined together.

I AM WORTHY ENOUGH

ATTRIBUTE 26

HE IS HUMBLE

> *By the Grace of God, I decree that your husband will be humble and allow God to do what he is not able to do.*

The Bible says in James 4:16 that, "God resist the proud but gives grace to the humble." A lot of men are very proud.

But a man who is humble knows when he needs to step back, let go of the arrogance and pride, and totally submit matters to God that he is trying to deal with and fix on his own. He will not try to assume the position of

God and do things his way. He knows that God is the One in full control of his life and not himself.

He will not allow any obstacles to hinder him from receiving all that God has for him and his family—not one single thing.

ATTRIBUTE 27

HE IS DISCIPLINE

> *By the Grace of God, I decree that your husband will be discipline in every area of his life.*

I have learned over the past few years of being married to a man that's in the ministry how important it is to be disciplined. Although I have been in the ministry too for years, even before I met my husband, I have been able to glean from him some things that helped me to become even more disciplined in certain areas of my life.

He is disciplined in his prayer life. He is disciplined in studying and reading the Bible. He is discipline in being on time for church and other events. He is disciplined in taking care of his family. He is discipline in his giving. He is disciplined in other areas of his life too.

I believe that God honors a man who is discipline because he knows that He can count of him to carry out certain tasks for Him and for his family. He knows that he is going to consistently strive to not only grow spiritually, but in every area of his life.

And a man who desires to grow closer to God, will be strengthen and become even more discipline in every area of his life.

I AM WORTHY ENOUGH

ATTRIBUTE 28

HE IS ONE OF A KIND

> *By the Grace of God, I decree that your husband will be one of a kind; one who cannot even be compared to any man that you have dated in your past.*

There is something unique about every human being. It is a person's uniqueness that sets them apart from someone else. They cannot easily be compared to anyone else because of that one particular thing that makes them totally different.

When I met my husband, I knew there was something so special about him. Not long after we met, we were at the altar saying, "I do." God had already ordained and sealed our union in Heaven before we first laid eyes on each other. I could not even begin to compare him to any other man I dated in my past, because God specifically allowed me to see Him inside of him, and assured me that he was one of a kind—the one that He handpicked and reserved for me.

The man that God has handpicked to be your husband is also one of a kind. There is something unique and special about him that won't even allow you to compare him to any other man that you dated in your past either.

Because of who he is in God, the fear that he has for God and that "something" special that was placed within his spirit at birth, you will no doubt embrace and receive him with open arms, having confidence that he will build you up and not tear you down. He will compliment you on your worst day. He will hug and kiss you when you don't even feel like you have been the best wife. He will apologize if he makes a mistake. He will treat you like the queen that you are every single day.

I AM WORTHY ENOUGH

ATTRIBUTE 29

HE HAS FAVOR WITH GOD

> *By the Grace of God, I decree that your husband will be favored by God all the days of his life.*

It is such a huge blessing when a man already has favor on his life. The Bible tells us that when a man finds a wife…he obtains favor from the Lord. (Proverbs 18:22). This is a sure and true Word from God that will no doubt manifest in a man's life when he finds his wife. It is a promise.

I can attest to the favor that He has shown my husband since we have been married. I have literally watched my husband experience back to back blessings from the Lord, and such uncommon favor in so many areas of his life. I have seen God open doors for my husband that I know only He could have done. And to witness this lets me know that "favor is not only fair," but it is real.

God allowed me to see that I was the reason that He has shown so much favor to my husband. It is not because I have been so good; it is because God was faithful to His word when He said the man will obtain favor when he finds a wife. When my husband found me, He found favor with God. And, that will apply to your husband when he finds you.

ATTRIBUTE 30

HE VALUES YOUR WORTH

> *By the Grace of God, I decree that your husband will value your worth; one who will appreciate the precious gift that you are to him.*

You are beautiful and "you were fearfully and wonderfully made." You are valuable to God. "Your worth is far above rubies." You are worthy of His best, and He wants you to have nothing less than His best.

When a man values his woman's worth, it shows that he appreciates God for the precious gift she is in his life. And that's just the kind of man God has for you. A man who will be thankful for the gift and take care of the gift called: you. He will honor his vows and love you from the crown of your head to the soles of your feet, throughout your marriage.

YOUR PERSONAL DECLARATION AND PRAYER REQUEST TO GOD ABOUT THE GODLY MAN YOU DESIRE

("Write the vision and make it plain")

_____

_____

_____

_____

_____

_____

_____

_____

_____

_____

_____

_____

_____

_____

I AM WORTHY ENOUGH

I AM WORTHY ENOUGH

I AM WORTHY ENOUGH

I AM WORTHY ENOUGH

I AM WORTHY ENOUGH

I AM WORTHY ENOUGH

I AM WORTHY ENOUGH

I AM WORTHY ENOUGH

I AM WORTHY ENOUGH

CPSIA information can be obtained
at www.ICGtesting.com
Printed in the USA
BVOW06s0123051216
469793BV00009B/179/P